A Nightmare's Daydream

Nia Mendonca

BookLeaf Publishing

India | USA | UK

Presentation by *BookLeaf Publishing*

Web: www.bookleafpub.com

E-mail: info@bookleafpub.com

ISBN: 9789358735246

First edition 2023

To my parents,

Janet and Rajesh,

and my sister,

Gia,

who always support me in anything I do.

I will always be grateful to you guys (yes, even you, Gia).

PREFACE

Warning!
This book contains references to murder, suicide, depression, blood, and anxiety. Such depictions can be triggering, so please take a second to place the book down and breathe if this happens. If you feel you cannot proceed in the story, then please put it away and go do something more uplifting. Sometimes, even as the author, I too, need to do the same.

-Nia Mendonca

Introduction

1983.
Not a sound,
Not a squeak,
Silence profound,
Echoing through the town.

Lights, flickering dim,
Till the last switch is thrown.
The town rests, an assured sleep.
No chance of interference,
In his murderous scheme.

This town, he now despises,
Though he once called it home.
The old orphanage that defined it,
Set to be demolished- taped off, closed.

Slinking along, through the night,
Carried by muscle memory.
Slipping like a shadow past suburban houses,
Down, down, to the dilapidated home,
That lay in haphazard splinters and peeling paint
At the end of the street.

Broken,

Torn,
Ripped in two.
A mirror of this stalker-
Murderer,
Killer.
Born from a life so, so cruel.

All it takes is a push,
A shove,
For everything to come crashing down.
A mother, father, son, brother-
What once was loved-
No longer.

Number Games

1, 2, 3
Hurting, bleeding, trying to breathe,
Drowning in the memories.

4, 5, 6,
A face full of life,
The smile of a kid.

7, 8, 9,
Playing with his friends,
The neighborhood orphans,
Sharks that grin as they gather around.

10, 11, 12,
A push, a shove,
That's all it takes.
A fall, a shout,
A brother's body on the ground.

13, 14, 15, 16.
Breathe, breathe, try to breathe,
No, no! I don't like the fours!
It's bad luck, this number scheme!
Go back to numbers divisible by three!

17, 18, 19, 20,
Who did it?
Why did they do it?
The world has no clue.
But jealousy can be a plague,
When you're an orphan,
And your "friend" isn't too.

21, 22, 23, 24
Everything? No, no,
Not anymore.
No more point in them being jealous,
When gone is the thing they longed for.

Gone is my brother,
Off a cliff,
Deceased is my father,
From a truck that slipped.
Dead is my mother,
Through a rope and a wall,
Deranged and murderous,
The brother that lived through it all.

25, 26, 27, 28, 29, and 30
Breathe, breathe.
We're back to three.
My family may be gone,
But the little child murderers can still experience
agony.

Death's Confidant

The swish of a cloak,
A whisper of fright.
Lifeless, paralyzing silence
That niggles at the back of the throat.

Longing for what was,
Guilt for what has been done.
A child's face, flitting through a memory,
Swallowed down in instinct.

One look- she should have known.
She should have seen the blankness in his gaze,
This man under her mistletoe.

Never should have let him in,
Never should have felt pity for that little boy's
facsimile,
For when she answered death's knock,
Now, she would never leave.

Dagger, cleaned and sharpened,
Aching for blood,
Exits its sheath
Quiet as a mouse.

That man in black,
Death's confidant,
Silent, deadly,
Unforgiving,
Seething.

Exercising his claws,
Even as death warns this unsuspecting victim.
"Run."
"Run."

"Turn around,
Don't come back.
Take your family,
Or skulls will crack.
Run, little bunny,
My friend seeks vengence.
Once he has you-
Your family too-
You'll see nothing but my eyes-
Bottomless,
Fathomless,
Black as midnight.
For a long.
Long.
Time."

Alas! My warnings,
Left unheard.

Now it is too late.
I warned you to run, little bunny.
Your death would be meaningless,
To him, nothing more than bait.
But nothing can be done.
Say your goodbyes.

One body.
Two bodies.
Red body.
Dead body.

Mouths-
Gaping,
Open in silent moans.
Stomachs-
Ripped, sliced open,
As blood flows freely in the snow.

No struggle,
No clues,
Nothing but a piece of paper,
With a rose so blue.

Futures are never certain,
But one thing is for sure.
When death comes knocking…
Best leave the door closed.

Infamy and Fortune

I'll linger at the borders,
Flitting through their memories.
Their nightmares,
I will star in-
Skirting the fringes of their dreams.
Just as they did…
To me.
To my family.

Like a movie,
It will be.
Directed, written, shot-
By me.
Oh! That was a pun,
Did you laugh?
Did you see?
I know I sure did,
It was extremely funny.
Tee hee.
Hee.
Hee.

Every scene will have a villain-
A victim,
My brother

And a hero-
Me!

Displayed in gruesome detail,
In all its macabre glory-
The murder of a child,
An innocent life- taken.
And the story of revenge,
Done by the brother of the one so dead.
To hurt the killers.
To shake the unshaken.

But with such an endearing show,
Comes fame and fortune.
Infamy- I hope to achieve…
For how else must I instill anxiety?

As for fortune, well,
I have no need for it.
No want for it.
No, I hate it.

Because fortune is what caused this…
Pain,
Hurt,
Death.
My family was fortunate, we had money,
We had love.
But when all is said and done?

Where do we stand?
Or should I say,
Where do we lay?
For at the end of the day…?
Only one of us still walks atop the land.

So forgive me when I say,
Fortune does not appeal to me.
From the morning after my brother's death,
When I awoke,
To the present day,
Nothing carries greater need in my heart,
Than that of retribution.

Because what good will riches do,
For a man who's very soul…
Is broke in two?

Children of Depravity

A sunrise stroll,
A walk in the dog park,
Happy, but he does not know
Who stalks him from the shadows…
Watching,
Waiting.

"A new serial killer runs rampant,
The Blue Death, he is called.
His first victims were found in the suburbs.
Police advise civilians to stay inside
Until this killer unknown
Can be identified,"
The newpapers publicize.

At the victims names,
His fingers tremble-
The first signs of fear.
When recognition flashes across his face,
He drops the paper,
And sprints to his home as if the hounds of hell
are on his heels.

At his door, he stands,
Fumbling with his key and the lock.
Breathing, panting, hyperventilating,
Life, flashing before his eyes,

At the sound of death's knock.

Inhale, exhale,
Blink,
Breathe,
Child of depravity.

Eight lives for one,
A steep price to pay,
But as beauty lies in the eyes of the beholder,
So does a person's worth differ
From every person questioned,
Each and every day.

A meal at sunset,
Doors- shut and locked.
His dog- barking, warning the man-
To the end, a loyal pet.

But closed shutters and a few locked doors?
At this point, its merely insulting.
Easy work made of the bolt,
Easy work made of the living.

His screams will satisfy,
But only to some end,
The girl must beg,
The girl must cry,
For this killer's bloodthirst to be quenched.

A Betrayal So, Very Painful

Two down, on to three,
Five more to go.
Stalking my next victims,
And they do not even know…

"The Blue Death",
They have named me.
Flattered, I should be,
But I am nothing if not angry,
Frustrated,
Aggrieved.

Why am I named the serial killer?
Why do they label me as crazy?
Why do they call me a criminal…
When they are the ones who refused justice for
my family?

Brother, father, mother, all gone-
In the blink of an eye.
And the memories of that day, so vivid,
They still arise in my mind.

As evening fell,
That fateful day,

My brother and I did as we had always done-
We threw open our door,
Excitement on our lips,
And flew out onto the street to play.

The summer heat was oppressive,
And my brother loved to joke,
That if we stuck out our tongues,
They would shrivel up,
Burnt to a crisp- cooked.

The air would dance,
Waltzing, shuffling,
As if trying to escape itself,
And its own blistering warmth.

It was days such as this one,
When we would escape our "prison"…
Warm, manicured lawns,
And yard flamingoes that stood,
Paint melting.

Mere minutes later,
Skirting the borders of the town,
Running to the promise of a swim.
"A secret place," whispered a turncoat-
A traitor neither of us knew about.

Dust bloomed in flowers in the air when we
would run,
Sweat tracked lightning bolts of water on our
faces,
Dripping in our eyes,
Soaking our hair.

She took us to a precipice,
One that rose high,
Mighty,
Reaching up to the firmament like the Tower of
Babel.

The cliff looked dauntingly upon us,
Pebbles slipping down its serrated slope.
A climb pockmarked by rocks sharp as daggers,
A fall guaranteed to be fatal.

Butterflies became locusts,
And unease became my mind.
The summer heat blurred my vision,
And my body felt like a hive.

But when I voiced my concerns,
She turned and laughed-
Laughed when I told her of the dangers,
The lurking, stalking feeling of death.

And at that time?

Her voice sounded like the water
 in the river that rushed below…
As it raced across the rocks.
It sounded like the gale in my hair…
Weeks before the winter's first frost.

But now?
I realize too late,
I should have listened to death…
When he whispered in my heart.
Because in reality?
Her voice was the wheezing rattle of a man's last
breath,
Gasping,
Dying.
It was the musical clatter of bones,
Click,
Clack,
As they fall to the ground, dust flying.

When her eyes gleamed,
I lost myself in them.
In my yearning for her, I overlooked the fact
That her eyes might not shine from her laughter,
But from her desire for pain and mayhem.
My pain.
My family's pain.

She shattered me that day,

And so, out of them all,
All those children,
All those sociopaths,
It is she that I search for in the world's sea of
people,
For it is she that I condemn.

The Federal Bureau of Investigation

7 investigators,
Gathered in a room.
Circular table,
With the evidence and the clues.

Physical evidence of the killer's identity,
They might be lacking.
But the sites of the deaths speak volumes,
And with much brain-racking,
The Blue Death's patterns,
His motives-
Vengeance? Psychosis?
Love? Anger?-
Can be discovered.

This team of seven,
Each with their own specialty,
Scavenge for clues,
Inspecting the crime scenes.

Who is this man
Stuck in his own head?
Who is this man
Who bats not an eye

at the sight of death?

Who is this unsub?
How does he think?
How does he act?
How does he speak?

Where does he come from?
Does he have an accent?
A scar? A disability?
Anything that can identify him?

So many questions,
So few answers.
Check the victims' histories,
Scour their houses.
See if anything can be found
To point in the right direction.

A death in the past?
Both victims were involved?
The dead boy's brother
Left alone,
his entire family gone?

This is the clue,
This is the lead,
This is the one they
so desperately need.

A suspect is found,
Now commence the search!
For it is him that they must retrieve.

Shakespearean Tragedies

Easy work it is,
To watch the unsuspecting.

They're always punctual,
Right on time.
Schedules so exact,
Simple to memorize.

It is what I hoped for,
Every stalker's dream-
A victim that is organized-
Easy pickings for predators like me.

They're all so stereotypical,
Child's play to predict.
Work so droll from 9 to 5,
Head for a drink with friends in the night,
No qualms about what if…
No qualms about what might.
Just working, talking, and drinking away their
lives.

Then again,
I wouldn't expect
Them to understand
The value of life.

Such a fleeting, fickle thing,
Our lives are.
Because of how simple it is
For one to be alive,
Living before your eyes,
Then gone in a blink,
Dead before you may even realize.

Unfortunately,
for fatalities three and four
And five and six,
I must join the melee,
And become what I most abhor.

I must blend in with the crowd,
Take suspicions off me,
I must get a job,
Make money,
And attend meet and greets.

Disgusting,
But I do what I must.
If vengeance means partaking in such nonsense,
I will throw myself in such a role so fully-
A role of laughter, drinking, and happiness-
One would never even realize
My childhood was such a Shakespearean
tragedy.

Bungle and Rye

Bungle and Rye,
Corruption spread wide,
House of scheming,
Coverups, and lies.

Lawyers that meddle,
Attorneys that tamper,
Courthouses oblivious,
Never the wiser.

This interview candidate
In a suit and tie,
Exudes confidence
In his eyes, in his stride.

Yet it's funny how
This young man's journey,
Takes him to a case
From 1953.

A child was murdered-
Pushed off a cliff.
The police asked questions,
But the evidence was gone
With a little extra payment.

No witnesses, none at all-
Except the boy's brother.
But since one is not a lot,
This made the work simpler,

Questions were asked,
Arrests were made,
Interrogations were done,
Yet not one of the killers caved.

The brother testified in court,
but his account was deemed false.
Bungle and Rye had cleaned up the evidence-
All the incriminating stuff-
Gone

Alas! Their past has come to haunt them,
The rabid puppy that they set loose,
Has come to bite them…
And leave a gaping wound.

This man all dressed up
In a suit and a tie,
With a calm, friendly, and happy exterior
Is maniacal, delirious, and demented inside.

Memory Lane

An outcropping, there was,
One which we were using
As our makeshift diving board,
Regardless of the consequences.

If our parents had come to know
That we came here to dive,
We would all be in trouble-
Grounded for life.

Looking back now,
Grounding would be the best
Outcome of that day
When I lost my dearest friend.

They dared him to jump
From the top, the peak.
I begged him to not,
"Don't do it," I pleaded.

Was it hubris?
Likely so.
But his death was murder,
That I know.

She followed him up there,
To ensure he would not run,
But when he readied himself on the edge of the
cliff,
He never got his chance to jump.

She nudged him, so slightly,
But it was enough
To alter his trajectory
And make him slam into the rocks.

I still remember-
His dead body arched,
Javelin-like rock
Running through his stomach.

The heart in my chest
Stopped beating that minute forward.
My mind could not even comprehend
What had just happened.

Police arrested us all,
Took us for interrogation.
Tried to make the other kids talk,
As they continued their investigation.

My own parents did not believe me.
These children we helped feed,
We helped to clothe,

We cleaned.
How could they do this?
They wouldn't!
They didn't do it!
But the truth is always hardest to believe.

I grieved alone for days,
Stuck in my own brain.
Guilt weighing me down,
Along with the anger in my parents' broken
gazes.

But their fury
Is nothing against mine.
No matter who believes me,
I know who committed the crime.

So she lied when she said
That she truly forgave me
For dating her sister
And loving her superficially.

She took my whole family,
That girl that I loved.
Because I made one mistake,
One single slip up.

Though at the end of the day,
She is at my mercy.

I will watch her plead with me-
On her knees-
When I go to make her pay.

Brand New Puppets

This stranger, man,
Dressed in a tie and suit.
Has not an ounce of work experience,
And no records from school.

The accepted him, this man,
Against their original beliefs.
They hired him, ignored the danger,
Even even as they understood subconsciously
That he would be their doom.

But their worries, he soon placated.
It wasn't even a year since he started his job
Looking for some money,
That he won employee of the month
And all the awards succeeding.

The ice around him broke,
Giving way for new " fellowships",
Invitations to the nearby pub-
Requested by friends,
Or in his mind, his brand new puppets.

But what is it he thinks?
What keeps him coherent,

When he has to make small talk
With people that numb his brain?

It is the thought, the idea, the very notion,
That when all is said and done?
Bungle and Rye will be screwed over,
Right to their rotten core.

And as employee of the month?
He sneaks into office, with but a flashlight,
gloves,
And his employee lanyard.
He will watch them collapse, stumble, fall
Into the pile of bullshit
That they really are.

What made them hire him?
Guess we'll never know.
But with him on the loose,
This case has now been broken
Wide, wide open.
And till the police come to a conclusion,
It won't be closed.

A Game of Death

My mind feels dimmed
From the sheer amount
Of idiocy and hubris
I've had to endure.

I have accepted every invitation
Because they do too.
Four of the murderers
Work for these crooks.

I sit through every conversation
With a look of mild interest
When in reality, my mind is elsewhere
Creating and adjusting my plans.

At the end of these meet and greets,
Each goes their own way.
I follow each one on their paths home
Each and every day.

I memorize every route,
Plan out every exit,
Map out the simplest passage
To find their safe havens,
So I can burn them to the ground

And torture them as they watch.

It's not very simple, however,
Staying under their radars.
Murdering someone can do that to a person,
No matter how cold their heart.

Their eyes dart everywhere,
Scanning the darkness
Searching for the suspicious shadows
That could be lingering anywhere

Each of their mansions
Are built in a different direction.
Filled with luxuries,
Dripping with money.

Each in their own
Secluded little circle,
With a formidable gate
Barring me from entering.

I am playing a dangerous game,
On a tricky board.
In this game of death, I must be careful
If I want to score.

So, I do what must.
I invite each to a party,

Held at the pub,
Drinks on me.

What they don't know,
Is that the afterparty
Will be at my house.
And they'll be so drunk,
That this time,
Oh, this time,
They will be at my mercy.

Iced Minds

A white powder
Disguised as fine sugar,
Shoved into a jean pocket,
Hidden from any onlookers.

A stranger, a man-
Dressed in a sweatshirt and jean pants-
Walks into a pub,
Carrying chloroform and intentions so bad.

The five of them order their drinks,
The man and his four victims,
John, they call him,
A false alias- not really his name.

They drink till inebriated,
Then drink a little more.
And when the time is just right,
They drink a little powder.

Enough to make them sway,
Till they are just slightly conscious.
Now at this man's mercy,
He laughs and grabs them.

And at the bartender's concerned stare,
He chuckles drunkenly, slurring his speech,
Swaying a little himself, he says,
"My friends must be quite tipsy!"

Shoving them in his car,
Binding their hands and feet.
Zip ties gleaming in the dim light,
As his victims slump forward in their seats.

He buckles them in with care,
Making sure not to cause too much harm.
He would not want them to die on the ride-
If they did, where would be the fun?

The ride is harsh and bumpy,
Strife with potholes and lumps,
The victims shudder with every breath,
Trying in vain to shout.

But their brains are sluggish,
Their thoughts- unable to align.
They truly try, but cannot think
With their frozen, iced minds.

The Blue Death

By the time we get back
To my dilapidated apartment,
They four of them are lucid enough
To stumble along,
But still dazed enough to not fight it
When I grab their shoulders and shove.

I take a moment to savor their expressions-
Looks that are strife with terror.
It pleases some deep part of me,
It fills me with pleasure.

I take them to the deepest,
Darkest run of my house.
A place where I know
That no one outside
Will be able to hear a sound.

I chain them to the wall,
I shackle them in place.
I prepare the iron bar
That I'll stick right in their faces.
If they don't answer my questions
Before I have to kill them.

I demand for them to tell me
Where the she-devil hides.
The one that started this all,
The one that organized it.

At first they don't respond-
I don't even think they've realized.
Then I see it,
a flicker of recognition,
That has the fear in their eyes
Doubling in size.

"You," one whispers,
"You're the Blue Death.
The one that's been targeting us all,
The one that killed our friends."

I snap.
The bar connects.
My arm rings with the force of the blow,
As her head flies around with an ominous crack.

It stays like that- her neck-
Twisted almost 180 degrees.
And my only regret is
That I didn't even get to start the torture.

But she does not get to give me
The speech about killing friends

When that is exactly what they did
All those years back.

So no, I won't hear it.
Won't even acknowledge what she said.
I stare past her unblinking eyes
Into the living ones of the victim right next
To her cold, hard body.

In discontent, I sigh.
Such a wasted opportunity,
But three still remain.
I pull out my knife,
And under it, they bleed.

I watch in gleeful rapture
As they implore me,
As they plead.
And I stand, unmoving, as they whimper…
Then begin to scream.

Sins of the Brother

Summer, 1953.
A little boy died,
A mistake,
According to the files.

Coincidence, it cannot be-
The fact that this event
Connects each victim's life
To the one who is next.

And his sibling claimed it was murder,
Claimed that his brother would never be so
careless
As to climb to the top of that cliff
Without gauging the consequences.

Then he died. Now, nothing can be done.
The case of the child is for another,
Today is the day to solve
The sins of that child's brother.

And to the person,
The one that agents believe
Could be their killer,
On a little vengeance streak.

It takes multiple weeks,
To sort this much out,
But when they do,
Everything falls together.

Originally, they had to
Play a little guessing game
To try and predict
Who the Blue Death planned to kill
Next in his schemes.

But their game was cut short
When the next bodies were found.
And another look at the files told them
That he planned to kill two birds in one stone.

After a couple more days-
Or rather, about a week-
The address of two people,
Husband and wife,
Are retrieved.

Agents swarm to reach their house,
Rushing against the time, frantically.
To reach them both before this pair becomes
The Blue Death's newest casualties.

Retribution Is Sweeter Than Blood

My last two targets,
My final task.
Alas, brother!
Your vengeance is at hand!

I creep in through an open window,
Rushing for the kids.
Quietly, I smother their cries,
And lay their unconscious forms under the
window sill.

I gag them, then bind them,
But never do I harm them.
Not until I know for sure
That I can use her children against her.

I quietly unplug the landline,
Just to be safe.
Just in case my plan
To cut the phone lines
Didn't work.

I tap her shoulder,
Watch as she stirs,

I stick a sock in her mouth
As she shrieks in terror.

Her husband- he was there,
Another orphan; an old friend,
Now turned enemy-
Turns and tries to attack me.

But sleep muddles his actions,
And I shove him to the ground
Before binding them both
And dragging them down
To the living room.

There, I stand-
Watching them shake off their sleep-
With my cord, my bar,
And my dagger in hand.

"Why are you here?" She asks.
So she knows who I am.
Good. All the better for me
When I kill her with my bare hands.

Her breath shudders when I near,
My knife gleaming dangerously,
And when it drifts to her youngest child's neck,
Her breath catches.
Gotcha.

Without hesitation, I slice through the tendons
The muscle and gore,
I slice and dice till blood and viscera
Stain the patterned floor.

Sobs rack her bound body;
She screams and wiggles to get closer.
She doesn't get far before she faceplants
Right in her child's own gore.

The horror on her face as she realizes what just
happened,
The way she shuffles, as if disgusted by the
patches
Of blood and muscle sticking to her face.

I quickly dispatch
Her two other children,
One after the other
In a similar pattern.

Then for her husband,
She's been broken thousands of times over by
now,
Yet still, I go on.
Taking my time with her spouse.

When I'm done,

I take out her gag.
All she can do
Is whisper hoarsely,
"Why?"

"Why?!" I demand, my body trembling in anger.
"You ask why,
But after all this time,
You never sought to understand.

"You let them believe I was delirious!
You let them believe I was mad!
You let them believe I was crazy!"
I lean in close- grinning when she whimpers-
And I whisper,
"But now,
I actually am."

I take years to finish with her,
Cutting shallow cuts with my knife-
Enough to cause intense pain,
But not enough for her to die.

Not immediately at least, but when she does,
She slumps forward with a groan,
Then one last shuddering breath
And silence- nothing more.

Until the sounds of sirens,

Split the midnight air.
I stand up with my arms raised
When I have a revelation.

Revelations

Those painful howls,
Touched my mind,
My heart,
My soul-
That lonely, broken piece of me.

In my quest to avenge
My brother's murder,
I found myself;
My life's true purpose.

When I started,
I had every intention
To finish the deeds,
And give my brother his vengeance.

But facing down these cops,
I have a revelation-
Who will deliver the justice
To those who deserve it?
And cannot distribute it,
However much they desire?

I already have experience,
Quite a bit, if I am honest,

I could be…
A valuable asset to society,
Rooting out the depraved, immoral,
Criminal, and immodest.

Death's blade, I will be,
Executioner; judge; jury.
In his tracks, I will follow,
He shall sow; I will reap.

My suffering has made me pure;
Deity in my own right.
The wicked, I shall burn;
The immoral, I shall torture;
And all the while, before death will judge,
The good from the bad I shall discern.

Epilogue

Ten little monkeys jumping on the bed,
One fell off and shattered his head.
Not a suicide, but murder,
Organized.
So his older brother vowed to get revenge.

Eight little monkeys jumping on the bed,
Proud that they got away with their little
stratagem,
But ignorance is bliss, and ignorant they are,
Because one little monkey wants them all dead.

Ten little monkeys jumping on the bed,
Nine of them are murderers,
Nine of them are dead.
The older brother crept up behind them and said,
"No more monkeys jumping on the bed."

Heads are rolling,
Knives are swinging,
On the bed, the bodies are cooling.
Everyone has their little fun something,
This one finds that his is killing.

Blood is pooling,

Cooling,
Congealing.
Little red threads that are dripping,
Unspooling.
One little monkey jumping on the bed;
if a body moves, he slits its neck.

Eight little bodies collected on the floor,
Outside, in the night,
Police sirens roar.
But plans can decide to change
In the blink of an eye,
Especially when one receives revelations galore.

One little monkey, running from the bed,
Serial killer in reality,
Vigilante in his head.

But what happens next?
Much is to come.
Is his story over,
Or has it just begun?

www.ingramcontent.com/pod-product-compliance
Lightning Source LLC
LaVergne TN
LVHW050938200726
843508LV00011B/2379